2021 Long Weekend Guide

Andrew Delaplaine

NO BUSINESS HAS PAID A SINGLE PENNY OR GIVEN *ANYTHING* TO BE INCLUDED IN THIS BOOK.

Senior Editors - ***Renee & Sophie Delaplaine***
Senior Writer - ***James Cubby***

Gramercy Park Press
New York London Paris

Please submit corrections, additions or comments to
andrewdelaplaine@mac.com

MÉRIDA
(Mexico)
The Delaplaine Long Weekend Guide

TABLE OF CONTENTS

Chapter 1
WHY MÉRIDA?

There are two main cities in the Yucatan Peninsula, Mérida and Cancún. Each has its own unique attraction. Mérida is the old colonial capital of the region and by far the more interesting of the two cities, with its stunning architecture going back for generations. Promenading is a popular pastime here in Mérida. As you walk by the large houses with their pastel colors, passing horse-drawn carriages clip-clopping along the colorful streets, you'll be transported back in time. These houses are benefitting from a current surge in restoration projects.

The people here are proud of their cultural history. They are proud of the way their ancestors resisted the Spanish conquerors. Many of the Mayan customs persist culturally here today. They still use many Mayan words mixed in with their Spanish. Much of the cuisine is informed by Mayan traditions. Because the Yucatan is cut off by geography from the rest of Mexico, people in Mérida have a unique local history and colorful past. They still celebrate a holiday called “Hanal Pixas,” which mixes Catholic and Mayan traditions in a “Day of the Dead” commemoration. You’ll see Christian images like crucifixes right next to skulls and various sacrificial food offerings to the gods. Somehow, these two religions have managed to commingle to create a hybrid that preserves many elements of the past. (“Hanal Pixas” is celebrated the first two days of November: one day is for adults and the other is for kids.)

I've always thought that the Yucatan really ought to be its own country. It's so different from the rest of this sad, unruly, unlawful country.

In scary, dangerous Mexico, you'll find Mérida one of the safest cities in the whole country (and a lot safer than Cancún, by the way, and much less expensive). The restaurant and nightlife scenes are vibrant and happening.

Before Mérida was Mérida it was T'ho, a thriving Mayan city. In 1542 the Spanish conquistadors, led by Francisco de Montejo, conquered the city and renamed it Mérida after the Spanish town it reminded them of. Then the lovely chaps proceeded to demolish all the Mayan structures and used the stones to build the cathedral and other official buildings of Mérida. The cathedral, **Catedral de San Ildefonso**, still stands to this day, dominating a corner of the central plaza.

Mérida, called the White City after its limestone buildings, is a mix of the past and present, of Spanish and Mayan, of New World and Old World.

Totally unlike Cancún, which is completely defined by the tourist industry, Mérida maintains its own unique identity and culture. Despite a population of over a million people, Mérida has a small hometown feel. This can be attributed to a diligent effort to maintain its colonial aesthetic. There is, thankfully, a totally lack of tall buildings in the center of town. When the Olimpo Cultural Center was being built on the Grand Plaza, it was originally designed with an avant-garde façade; but public pressure mounted, and the government stepped in, forcing the adoption of a design more in keeping with the surroundings.

Mérida is one of the safest cities in Mexico. Expats love its laid-back feel, combined with a rich cultural heritage. There is a thriving community of snowbirds who come down from the colder climes of the US to enjoy the winter months in warm Mérida. There has always been a strong link between Mérida and the European Continent. Many of the tourists who choose Mérida are from Europe.

Méridianos are very social and culturally inclined and jealously guard the customs of the region. Where other cities of region are driven to entertain tourists, one gets a definite sense that Mérida's many entertainments are presented for the benefit of its own citizens. The horse-drawn calesas stationed at the corner of the Grand Plaza are just as likely to be filled by a local family as by foreigners. Every night of the week the city is offering traditional entertainment at one plaza or another.

Getting around the center of town is very simple, as Mérida uses a simple grid. Even streets run in order north-south, and odd numbered streets go east-west. Addresses are always given by street, number, and cross streets, making locating one's destination very easy.

There are several tourist offices downtown. The state has offices just inside the entrance of the **Palacio de Gobierno** on the plaza, as well as in the **Teatro Peón Contreras** on the corner of 60 and 57. The city also has an information center in the municipal center of the west side of the plaza. Once in town, we suggest you pick up a copy of the weekly **Yucatán Today**, which is written in English and Spanish, for a current listing of the shows and events being offered in town. They also have a website: www.yucatantoday.com.

RENTING A CAR

Renting a car is a great way to explore the many opportunities Mérida and the Yucatán Peninsula have to offer. We recommend reserving your car ahead of time. When renting your car, it is very important that

you specifically request insurance equal to the value of the car. It is not made clear when you pick up your car, but you are personally responsible for any damage to the car. Upon return you are at the mercy of the staff for any scratch, so be very aware of the condition of the vehicle when you get it.

HOTEL

Chapter 2
LODGINGS

Budget – Mid-Range – Luxury

Mérida has its share of large international hotel chains, such as Hyatt, Intercontinental, Fiesta Americana, Holiday Inn. These are all located in the same area, by the intersection of the Paseo Montejo and Calle Colon, about 15 minutes from the center of town. Tourists to Mexico spend over US$11 billion dollars a year, but much of that money goes to international conglomerates. We prefer to encourage you to give your money to local businesses, whose profits are spent in the community they reside in. Many of the hotels we list here are excellent local businesses that deserve your support. Go local -- go Mexico!

Budget

CASCADAS DE MÉRIDA
Calle 57 #593C x 74A y 76, Mérida: 52-999-923-8484/ 305-978-5855
www.cascadasdemerida.com
This is a small bed and breakfast – there are only four rooms. But what they lack in size they make up for in service. The owners Ellyne and Chucho are some of the most dedicated hosts you will ever find. The ambiance is flawless, the waterfalls are exquisite and set a serene mood for the whole site. Dedicated guests return here time after time.

HOTEL JULAMIS
Calle 53 #475B x Calle 54, Mérida: 52-999-924-1818
www.hoteljulamis.com
This popular retreat offers great personal service from owners Erid and Mel, who are extremely accommodating. A great full breakfast is included.

Prices are extremely good, particularly for the great service they offer.

HOTEL CASA CONTINENTAL
Calle 47 #480 x 56 Centro, Mérida: 52-999-924-1401
www.hotelcasacontinental.com
A newly remodeled small hotel near the center of town. They really make good use of the space. Most of the rooms are airy and bright – modern with flourishes of local color. They have some unique touches, like a retracting roof in the lobby. The service here is excellent – they treat their guests well. Great value for the price.

HOTEL DEL PEREGRINO
Calle 51 #488 x 54 y 56, Centro, Mérida: 52-999-924-3007, 1-888-988-2633
www.hoteldelperegrino.com
A consistently good small hotel – basic, but charming and clean, quiet and cool. Jim, the owner, and his staff are very friendly. They have a very dedicated core of return guests. Tip: ask for an upper room. Continental breakfast. The rooftop patio is a great place to enjoy the evening. There is always plenty of parking in front of the hotel.

HOTEL DOLORES ALBA
Calle 63 #464 x 52 y 54, Centro, Mérida: 52-999-928-5650
www.doloresalba.com
Large cool rooms, small cool pool. This is a good clean basic hotel located in the heart of downtown. Rumor is that they offer free beer in the pool area.

Mediocre continental breakfast, so step out the front door and find some good inexpensive eats. For those with a car, this place has safe, secure parking.

HOTEL ECLIPSE
Calle 57 #491 x 58 y 60, Centro, Mérida: 52-999-923-1600
http://hoteleclipsemerida.com.mx
Small inn with 14 rooms has a unique design idea: each room has a theme, as in "lava," "disco," etc. Cheap, but very nice.

HOTEL MAISON DEL EMBAJADOR
Calle 60 #472 x 53 y 55, Centro, Mérida: 52-999-928-1243/ 800-841-9496
www.maisondelembajador.com
This is a lovely hotel in the center of the city where you can enjoy good, clean rooms and strong hot showers. The pool area is particularly beautiful. The complimentary breakfast is the best you'll find in the city, with many hot and cold options to choose from.

They have a business center with plenty of computers available for use at any time.

HOTEL MEDIO MUNDO

Calle 55 #533 x 64 y 66, Centro, Mérida : 52-999-924-5472

www.hotelmediomundo.com

An utterly charming bed and breakfast near the center of town. The space is delightfully painted in those vivid colors we love to expect from Mexican Colonial. This place will not disappoint. The rooms and cheerful and stylish. The breakfast is ample and tasty. The staff will make you feel like it's your own home.

LUZ EN YUCATAN

Calle 55 #499 x 60 y 58, Centro, Mérida : 52-999-924-0035

www.luzenyucatan.com
Certainly one of the best places to stay in Mérida and excellent prices. The staff is friendly and helpful. Free cold beer when you check in, and shots of tequila whenever you want. Charming pool area. Plain street façade – as with most latin houses, all the charm is on the inside. The location is excellent, two blocks from the plaza.

MARIA DEL CARMEN HOTEL
Calle 63 #550 x 68 y 70, Colonia Centro, Mérida: 52-999-930-0390/ 800-712-0015
www.hotelmariadelcarmen.com.mx
A good basic hotel. Clean, quiet, and comfortable. Centrally located. Helpful staff.

SUITES DEL SOL
Calle 58 #405 x 39 y 41, Centro, Mérida: 52-999-923-6854/ 800-570-7510
www.suitesdelsol.com
Situated in the Paseo Montejo area, this is not a hotel per se, but rather apartment suites available for short or long-term stay. If you're staying in town for any period of time, this is an excellent affordable alternative to a regular hotel. The suites are clean and well-appointed. They come stocked with all you need to live comfortably, including full kitchen, air conditioning, wifi, etc.

Mid-Range Hotels

CASA MEXILIO GUEST HOUSE
Calle 68 #495 x 59 y 57, Mérida: 52-999-928-2505/ 888-819-0024
www.casamexilio.com
This unique offering is a converted 18th century mansion with lots of nooks and crannies to explore. The rooms and common areas are flawlessly decorated with original antiques. The roof is a wonderful place to enjoy the warmth of the sun or a cool tropical evening. Ignore the cats, for they shall ignore you. The owner, Roger, can be described as eccentric or even crotchety but actually is a very interesting person. The staff is efficient and courteous. If you are the sort of guest who needs a lot of special attention, this is probably not the place for

you. Breakfast in the gorgeous dining room is an event.

CASA SAN ANGEL
Montejo #1 x 49 Centro, Mérida: 52-999-928-1800
www.hotelcasasanangel.com
Quaint boutique hotel. An excellent value for the price. Wonderful attention to details gives the place a great 100% Mexican atmosphere. Even if you don't stay in this charming hotel, make a point to eat at the restaurant. The food is very good, with a surprising Asian/Indian influence. Locals know to come here regularly for the fine cuisine. Also, on Fridays, there's a free show for anybody who happens by: comedy, trova music, mariachi, marimba, folk dancing.

FIESTA AMERICANA MÉRIDA
Paseo de Montejo #451, Esquina Avenida Colón, Colonia Centro, Mérida: 52-999-942-1111/ 877-92 77666

www.fiestamericana.com
Another of the grand hotels in the business district. Certainly the most impressive building. The huge lobby is a fun place to see and be seen. The rooms and service are what you would expect from a five star hotel. Treat yourself and upgrade to the fiesta level, you'll really feel pampered. Great artisan shops on the arcade level. The lavish breakfast buffet is the perfect start for a day of sightseeing or business meetings. Both restaurants in the hotel are excellent.

GRAN REAL YUCATAN
Calle 56 #474 x 55, Centro, Mérida: 52-999-924-8268
www.granrealyucatan.com
One of the greatest things about this older hotel is the location. It is centrally located between the historic downtown and the Paseo Montejo. The rooms are spacious, clean and quiet with tile floors and antique-looking furniture.

HACIENDA MISNE
Calle 19 #172 x 6B, Mérida: 52-999-940-7150/ 866-507-0278
www.haciendamisne.com.mx
These people really know how to greet a guest in the sweaty tropics – with a smile and a tall cool glass of fresh-squeezed juice. The hotel sits on the edge of the city, and reflects an elegant combination of city and country. The rooms and the bathrooms are huge and very comfortable. The grounds and the multi-level pools are especially beautiful.

HOTEL HACIENDA MÉRIDA
Calle 62 # 439, Centro, 97000 Mérida, Yuc., 52-999-924-4363
www.hotelhaciendamerida.com
Well-appointed rooms. The owner, Alex, is from France and knows how to offer good service. Thus, the staff is unobtrusive yet helpful. The pool area is lovely and relaxing, and the pool actually is deep enough to really enjoy. They have an excellent bar in this hotel. The service is impeccable and the drinks are delicious.

HOTEL VILLA MARIA
Calle 59 #553 x 68, Colonia Centro, Mérida: 52-999-923-1727
www.vivameridahotel.com
A restored 17th century Mansion is the perfect setting for this stylish hotel. The outside busy streets seem miles away. The interior is tranquil. 11 suites open out onto the courtyard with a small pool. Each suite

has a large bathroom. The hotel restaurant is very good and an excellent value.

PIEDRA DE AGUA HOTEL
Calle 60 # 498 x 59 y 61, Centro, Mérida: 52-999-924-2300/ 800-999-924-2300
www.piedradeagua.com
WEBSITE DOWN AT PRESSTIME
This lovely converted mansion sits in the historic center of town, an excellent location less than a block from the central plaza. The décor here is really elegant. The patio area is really beautiful with a lovely view of the cathedral. A couple of the rooms are small, but for the most part they are spacious.

Luxury

HACIENDA XCANATUN
Calle 20 S/N x 19 y 19A, Mérida: 52-999-930-2140/ 888-883-3633
www.xcanatun.com
This hacienda is some distance on the outskirts of town, so it is rather isolated. However, the setting is so exquisite, you may never want to leave the grounds. Pictures don't do justice to this serene setting. Owners Jorge and Cristina are sweet and attentive. The grounds are impeccably groomed. The rooms and suites and large and comfortable, each with access to the terraces. The atmosphere somehow manages to be both contemporary and traditional. Two pools provide refreshment from the tropical heat. Of course, spa services are offered as well.

The hacienda factory, with its hi
converted into a restaurant and b
excellent, known for its Yucateca
frequented by locals in the know.

HOTEL HACIENDA VIP
Calle 62 441-A x 51 y 53, Centro, Merida: 52-999-924-4363/ 866-539-0036
www.hotelhaciendamerida.com
No effort is spared in making this a first-class luxury hotel. The rooms are spacious and elegant. The beds are swathed in Egyptian cotton sheets. The pool is elegant and beckoning. The service is impeccable. Even the songbirds are on board, providing a soothing mask for the bustle outside the insulating walls. Perfectly located in the center of town.

HACIENDA SAN JOSE
Km 30 Carretera Tixkokob-Tekanto, Tixkokob: 52-999-924-1333/ 800-325-3589

w.marriott.com/hotels/travel/midlc-
a-san-jose-a-luxury-collection-hotel-san-jose/
ated outside Mérida in the small town of
ixkokob, the Hacienda San Jose Cholul has everything to offer one who wants to get away from it all. You're never more than a few steps from an inviting hammock. The main house features rooms with lofty ceilings and exposed beams. Or you can choose a charming palapa-topped hut for more privacy. Lounge by the pools or let the helpful staff arrange for a horse ride. Enjoy the kiss of Mother Nature with an eco tour. Explore the local traditions with a visit to the Mayan village. Dining is an event here in the elegant restaurant or under lamp-lit trees.

HOTEL CASA DEL BALAM

Calle 60 #488 x 57, Colonia Centro, Mérida: 52-999-924-8844/ 800-624-8451
www.casadelbalam.com
Another fine converted mansion centrally located in the heart of downtown. The rooms are clean. The staff is friendly. For a quieter stay, ask for a room on an upper floor. They have a decent breakfast here, but for lunch or dinner we recommend one of the fine restaurants out in town.

HYATT REGENCY MÉRIDA

Ave. Colon esq Calle 60, Mérida: 52-999-942-1234
www.hyatt.com/en-US/hotel/mexico/hyatt-regency-merida/merid
A well-maintained corporate hotel. The rooms and spacious and clean. The staff is warm and courteous,

and most are bilingual. The large rooftop pool is a nice feature.

INTERCONTINENTAL PRESIDENTE MÉRIDA
Ave. Colon 500 Centro, Mérida: 52-999-942-9000, 888-424-6835
www.intercontinental.com
One of the better priced of the corporate hotels in the Montejo/Colon district, and, happily, one of the better run. The rooms are stylish, the beds are comfy, the food is good. The management is really on the ball at this hotel. If there are any problems, they will fix them immediately. The best rooms are high up overlooking the pool.

ROSAS AND XOCOLATE

Paseo de Montejo #480 x 41, Col.Centro, Mérida: 52-999-924-2992

www.rosasandxocolate.com

Absolutely the very best boutique hotel, they have all the details right. The space is a wonderful restoration of two old mansions from the 1930s on the historic Paseo de Montejo. The owner, Carol Kolozs, a real hands-on guy, has gone to great lengths to create a perfect environment – and he knows his wines! The décor is really quite excellent, inside and out with great architectural details. Wonderfully luxurious rooms (17 of them) with perfect comfy beds. Great spa – don't miss the lavender facial. (They even have a chocolate treatment in the Spa.) There is even a 24-hour chocolate shop in the lobby for that 3 a.m. craving. The restaurant and bar are popular with the locals, which is always a good sign. As one of the pricier lodgings in the area, they at least offer you a free full breakfast.

Chapter 3
RESTAURANTS

Budget

100% NATURAL
Healthy, Vegetarian, Vegan
Calle 8 #306 x 1 and 1A, Mérida: 52-999-948-4590
www.100natural.com.mx
100% Natural is a restaurant chain that is happily taking Mexico by storm. The food offered is free of preservatives and artificial flavors and colorings. For breakfast, lunch and dinner, healthy fare is the theme. The juice bar offers fresh made juices from local fruits and veggies. The delicious whole-wheat bread is baked fresh on-site, so try one of their tasty sandwiches. We recommend the veggie burger.

EL ARBOL
Vegetarian, Vegan
Calle 25 #182, Colonia Garcia Gineres, Mérida: 52-999-925-3849
NO WEBSITE
A tasty vegetarian restaurant with no set menu. They create a difference prix fixe meal each day. The meal includes salad, drink and dessert. The food is delicious, healthy and inexpensive.

EL TRAPICHE
Mexican
Calle 62 #491, Mérida: 52-999-928-1231
NO WEBSITE
A great basic restaurant that has a lot going for it. It is centrally located a few steps from the plaza. The food is delicious and the prices can't be beat. It's usually crowded, but the wait staff is efficient and friendly. Many locals and ex-pats come here regularly, if not daily. If you are in town for any period of time, we recommend you make El Trapiche a regular occasion for both lunch and dinner.

LA CHAYA MAYA
Yucatecan
Calle 62 X 57, Centro Historico, Mérida: 52-999-928-4780
www.lachayamaya.com
We have never passed this place without noticing that it is packed. From open to close, this place is full of people. The place is done up very colorfully, with eye-catching decorations and traditional uniforms for the wait staff. *This place is 100% authentic Yucatecan*. The service is busy but friendly, and you'll find the owner, Osman, working right alongside his staff. Locals, Latinos and gringos all flock to La Chaya, which is kind of like a diner. If you arrive after 1pm, expect to wait for a table. But you won't mind the wait because of the colorful carnival that is this restaurant. Enjoy watching traditional tortillas hand-made on a charcoal grill in the front window.

Once you've got your table, you'll be glad you waited. If you know your Yucatecan food you'll find all your favorites here. The Pibil dishes are superb. If this is your first time, try one of the generous combination platters. Or try the house creation, Los Tres Mosqueteros Yucatecos, or The Three Musketeers, which puts a plate of 3 local specialties in front of you: relleno negro, a dark sauce made with chiles that have been burned and lots of spices, served over pork; pipián, a turkey dish topped with a pumpkin seed sauce; and papadzul, made with eggs. (All this for just a few pesos.)

The food comes hot and fast, with large portions. With all this flash and color, you would expect it to be expensive, but the prices here are very good. For quantity, quality, and cost, La Chaya Maya can't be beat.

LO QUE HAY CAFÉ
HOTEL MEDIOMUNDO
Calle 55 533, Mérida, +52 999 924 5472
www.hotelmediomundo.com/index.php
CUISINE: International Vegan
DRINKS: No Booze
SERVING: Breakfast, Lunch, & Dinner; Closed Mondays
PRICE RANGE: $$
NEIGHBORHOOD: Parque Santa Lucia
Popular eatery (if you're vegan) serving different world cuisines and international vegan dinners. Very colorful setting in the hotel, or out by the refreshing pool. Fixed menu includes pastas, rice dishes, salads, pizzas and desserts. It's always different. You might

have Lebanese food one day, and Japanese the next. Free breakfast if you're a guest in the hotel.

LOS TROMPOS

Mexican

Calle 59 #502 x 60, Centro, Mérida: 52-999-988-4444

www.lostrompos.com.mx

This is another good Mexican food restaurant in the center of town. The Mexican dishes are tasty, as are the pizzas. The modern décor is spotlessly clean, the ambiance is bright and airy. Open for breakfast, lunch and dinner.

WAYAN'E STREET STAND

Circuito Colonias por 4-A 57-C, Felipe Carrillo Puerto, Mérida: 999 993 4606

It's a little out of the way, on the north side of town. But you'll love this little place where the Loris family has been serving up cheap foods (from breakfast on) for some 20 years. Tacos like you've never had them before, smoky chicken and pork fajitas, eggs scrambled with Swiss chard. You sit at a stainless steel counter and pay almost nothing for great local food.

Mid-Range

130 GRADOS STEAKHOUSE
Calle 47 465, Merida, +52 999 429 5398
www.130grados.mx
CUISINE: Steakhouse
DRINKS: Full Bar
SERVING: Lunch & Dinner
PRICE RANGE: $$$
NEIGHBORHOOD: Centro
Small elegant upscale steakhouse serving what some consider the best steaks in town. Most steaks are pretty big; some can serve 2 to 3 persons. Large choice of starters, including nice seafood items. Wide selection of prime cuts, from Cowboy steak to the Tomahawk. Superb grilled octopus. Excellent whiskey selection, especially among the single malts on offer.

AMARO
Yucatecan, Vegetarian, Vegan
Calle 59 #507 x 60 y 62 Centro Historico, Mérida: 52-999-928-2451
www.restauranteamaro.com
This great little restaurant has one of the best settings in Mérida. It is situated in the courtyard of an old building. Evening here is a wonderful romantic event, with candlelit tables, attentive waiters and live music. The food here is local Yucatecan fare with a heavy emphasis on vegetarian. They even have some vegan options. Dishes of note include the Sopa de Lima and the Avocado Pizza.

APOALA MEXICAN CUISINE
Calle 55 S/N, Merida, +52 999 923 1979
www.apoala.mx
CUISINE: Mexican
DRINKS: Full Bar
SERVING: Lunch & Dinner
PRICE RANGE: $$$
NEIGHBORHOOD: Centro

Elegant eatery with archways separating you from a courtyard providing a lot of atmosphere. Tile-topped tables. Has a stellar menu offering Mexican fare. Favorites: Octopus & Scallops ceviche and Grilled Shrimp. Speakeasy bar in the back.

BRYAN'S
116 between 5 & 7 Fracc
Chamber of Commerce Ave, Montecristo, +52 999 948 2034
www.bryansmerida.com
CUISINE: International/Contemporary
DRINKS: Full Bar

SERVING: Lunch, Dinner, Late Night
PRICE RANGE: $$
NEIGHBORHOOD: Montecristo
Modern eatery with an elegant interior, dark and intimate, offering a menu of International fusion cuisine. Favorites: Mixed seafood casserole with garlic (astounding flavors); Spaghetti Bryan's (with home-smoked chicken & peppers); Roast Beef sandwich au jus (like a French dip); Tuna carpaccio; Flat iron steak is served with a "salsa bordolasa" that's been reduced for 15 hours. Wonderfully flavorful. Great burgers, also. Ok wine list.

HACIENDA TEYA
Mérida-Cancún Hwy., km 12.5, Mérida: 52-999-988-0800
www.haciendateya.com

This is a short drive (15 to 20 minutes) outside town, but it's worth it because you'll get to have dinner in a plantation dating back to the 17th Century. It used to handle cattle, but the place was given over to rope making in the 19th Century. Go in plenty of time to enjoy the beautiful grounds. And be sure to take a few minutes to look at the vintage photos of "old Mérida" that date back 100 years or more. The food is simple but reflective of the local cuisine: cochinita pibil (citrus-marinated roasted pork), poc chuc (pork that's grilled after undergoing a marinade made from sour oranges). Start with the soupa de lima (chicken soup with an eye-opening dose of lime juice).

KUUK
Av. Romulo Rozo 488, Col. Itzimná, +52 999 944 3377
www.kuukrestaurant.com
CUISINE: Mexican
DRINKS: Full Bar
SERVING: Lunch & Dinner, Closed Mondays
PRICE RANGE: $$$
NEIGHBORHOOD: Centro
Modern eatery in a stately building offering a contemporary twist on classic Yucatán dishes. Lovely gourmet menu. Two options here: A Tasting Menu (which I heartily recommend unless there's something specific you really want) and an a la carte 'Menu for the Season'. Menu picks: Castakan con Queso (Pork Belly and with Cheese); Suckling Pig (cooked for 3 days in lentil stew); Lengua (Beef Tongue). Extensive Mexican wine and tequila list.

LA RUEDA
Calle 37 352- A, Col. Emiliano Zapata
Mérida, +52 999 944 4584
No Website
CUISINE: Steakhouse/Argentinean
DRINKS: Full Bar
SERVING: Lunch & Dinner, Closed Mondays
PRICE RANGE: $$
NEIGHBORHOOD: Chem Bech
Casual Gaucho themed Argentinian style steakhouse with great meats and prices to match for the quality you get. Wide selection of cuts. Favorites: Goat empanadas and Beef filet. Delicious Kobe burger (served only in the evenings). Nice cocktails. Note: non-English speaking staff. But order beef and maybe a Caprese and you'll be fine.

OLIVA ENOTECA
Calle 47 & Esquina con 54 S/N, Mérida, +52-999-923-3081
www.olivamerida.com
CUISINE: Italian
DRINKS: Full Bar
SERVING: Lunch & Dinner; Closed Sundays
PRICE RANGE: $$$
NEIGHBORHOOD: Parque Santa Lucia/Centro
Located in an old house lovingly updated with shiny metal seats at the bar and black-and-white checked tile on the floor is this upscale eatery offering Italian haute cuisine. Don't eat too many of the breadsticks or you won't have room for the delicious pastas they serve up. Favorites: Steak tartare; a very nice beef carpaccio; Risotto alla Milanese with Brasato; and

k pasta. Great cocktails and impressive selection
f Mexican wines.

Expensive

HENNESSY'S IRISH PUB
Bar Food, English, Irish, Fusion
Paseo de Montejo Calle 56-A #486-A, 41 y 43, Col. Centro, Mérida: 52-999-923-8993
www.hennessysirishpub.mx
Some might question the authenticity of an Irish pub in Mexico, but fear not, the owners here run a right Irish pub, and the ambience is perfect. The drinks are ice cold and the patrons friendly. They have a good selection of rare Irish whiskeys. This is a popular hangout for the local expats. There are five different areas, each with a different theme, such as the salon or the Irish writers' room.

But don't just go for the drinks – the food here is also a treat. They have an extensive menu full of standard bar fare done up right, but also some really delicious specialties from the British Isles. The Irish

Stew is not to be missed. A bit pricey; but factoring in all the touches, we'd say it's worth it.

This place is one of the hottest spots in town, believe it or not. Just have a look at how fast the terrace outside fills up after the sun goes down.

LA BIERHAUS

German

Calle 62x 57 y 59 487, Centro, Mérida, 52-999-928-0333

http://labierhaus.com

As the name would imply, there are many beers available here. You will find a good selection of both Mexican and German beers, and well as come very good German wines. The menu offers many interesting options. There are a variety of different sausages to choose from. We recommend the Wursteller, which has a sampling of everything. The house specialty is the Chamorro, a slow-roasted pork.

LA CASA DE FRIDA

Mexican, Vegetarian

Calle 61 #526-A x 66 y 66-A, Mérida: 52-999-928-2311

The décor in this sweet little place is wonderful. Bright pink walls glow with Mexican hospitality. Chef Gabriela Praget created it as an homage to Frida Kahlo. The dishes reflect a love and dedication to traditional Mexican food. The Chiles en Nogada must be tried. They offer a nice selection of vegetarian options. The service leaves something to be desired, but the food makes it worth it.

LA PIGUA

Seafood

Calle 33 #505-A between Cupules and 62, Mérida: 52-999-920-1126, 52-999-920-3605

www.lapiguamerida.com

A nice, upscale place for seafood. The seafood is bought fresh from local fishermen. It's all delicious. The seafood-stuffed catch of the day is always perfect. The signature dish here is the Coco Shrimp, which is now copied by many other establishments. For dessert look no further than the exquisite coconut pasteles de tres leches, or wait, the coconut ice cream!

LA RECOVA

Argentinian BBQ

Prolongacion Montejo #382 x 33 y 35, Mérida: 52-999-944-0215

www.larecovamerida.com

Here is where the carnivores come to get their fill, and we mean fill, of meat. Argentinians know their meat like most nobody else, and here they do not disappoint. Portions are huge. Even the desserts are huge … and delicious. Delicious grilled veggies and some tasty pasta dishes are available for those who don't prefer meat.

LA TRATTO
Italian
Calle 60 No.471 x 53 y 55, Local 10, Centro, Mérida, 52-999-923-3787
www.latrattomerida.com
Delicious pizza the authentic Italian way. The pasta, as one would expect, is excellent. And be not to miss the freshly baked bread. It's hard not to talk about the bar, which dominates the setting with a 20-foot-high mirrored wall of alcohol. Of course the drinks are tasty.
6pm – 3am

LOS ALMENDROS
Yucatecan
Calle 50-A 493, Centro, Mérida: 52-999-928-5459
www.restaurantelosalmendros.com.mx

Located in the lobby of the Fiesta Americana hotel, you'll see many locals enjoying their favorite Los Almendros creations. This is part of a chain of restaurants which really put Yucatecan food on the map. They are known for their Poc-Chuc, a pork skirt steak dish. Another all-time favorite is the Cochinita Pibil. The service is excellent, which one expects of a five-star hotel.

NECTAR
Av. Andrés García Lavín 329, Mérida, +52 999 938 0838
www.nectarmerida.com.mx
CUISINE: International/Mexican
DRINKS: Full Bar
SERVING: Lunch & dinner; closed Sun
PRICE RANGE: $$$$
NEIGHBORHOOD: Merida
Elegant upscale eatery offering a classic take on local Yucatecan cuisine. Very nice seating outside with some plants and vines hanging from beams overhead. Favorites: Carbon Octopus; Black Onions (don't ask, just get them if available); and Short Rib Taquitos. Impressive wine list. Delicious locally inspired desserts. Reservations recommended.

PANCHO'S
Mexican
Calle 59 x 60 y 62, Mérida: 52-999-927-0434/ 52-999-923-0942
www.panchosmerida.com
This place gets a lot of mixed reactions. It is a theme restaurant of the Mexican revolution. All the waiters

are dressed like Pancho Villa. The walls are covered in period tcshotskes. The words "tourist trap" have been used in conjunction with Pancho's more than a few times. The kids will probably love it. The food isn't bad, and the portions are generous. The Cowboy Ribeye Steak is so big you might need to bring it home. Or you can just bring home a t-shirt – they sell them at the counter.

ROSAS AND XOCOLATE
Paseo de Montejo #480 x 41, Col. Centro, Mérida:
52-999-924-2992
www.rosasandxocolate.com
The restaurant inside this trendy hotel is really good: the duck comes with corn that been singed, sausage and a melon compote. Or try the fish of the day served on a fried tortilla with a side pear salad that's a great taste combination.
There is even a 24-hour chocolate shop in the lobby for that 3 a.m. craving. The restaurant and bar are popular with the locals, which is always a good sign.

SIQUEFF RESTAURANT
Lebanese, Middle Eastern
Calle 60 #350 x 35 y 37, Mérida: 52-999-925-5027
www.siqueffrestaurant.com
A tasty place to find good Middle Eastern food. Try the Kafta, Kibi or Tabouli. The Fried Chicken is also very good. The Siqueff family has a long tradition of serving food in the Yucatan. They created the popular Huevos Motulenos for the governor in the 1920s.
8am – 6pm

TROTTERS
Steaks, Seafood, Tapas
Calle 31 #134 entre Calle 34 y Calle 36, Buenavista, Mérida: 999-927-2320
www.trottersrestaurants.com
A mainstay of high-end dining in Mérida, Trotters has a lovely, elegant ambience that cannot be described, only seen.

Chapter 4
NIGHTLIFE

MAMBO CAFÉ
Plaza Las Americas Shopping Mall. 52-999-987-8787
www.mambocafe.com.mx
Mambo Café is a legend in Mérida. Here is where you come when you want to Salsa the night away to excellent live music.

HOTEL CASA SAN ANGEL
Montejo #1 x 49 Centro, Mérida: 52-999-92-08-00
www.hotelcasasanangel.com
On Fridays, there's a free show for anybody who happens by: comedy, trova music, mariachi, marimba, folk dancing. Get a seat on the terrace and enjoy the show. Quaint boutique hotel. An excellent value for the price. Wonderful attention to details gives the place a great 100% Mexican atmosphere. Even if you don't stay in this charming hotel, make a point to eat at the restaurant. The food is very good, with a surprising Asian/Indian influence. Locals know to come here regularly for the fine cuisine.

PIEDRA DE AGUA HOTEL
498 – 60th St, Mérida: 52-999-924-2300
www.piedradeagua.com
WEBSITE DOWN AT PRESSTIME
There's a bar outside this hotel that has impressive views of the lighted façade of the cathedral towers. Try to be there on a Friday night when you can hear jazz and blues groups play. You'll drink lemon daiquiris, of course with basil leaves, or the ubiquitous mojitos. Order a pizza that has an unusual topping called huitlacoche, which is a corn fungus. (Trust me, it's not what you think.)

TEQUILA ROCK
Prolongacion Montejo #248C x 1-C and Ave. Campestre. 52-999-944-1828/ 52-944-2477
Popular dance club featuring djs and hot pop music.

Chapter 5
ATTRACTIONS

WEEKLY EVENTS

MONDAY

At 9pm the Palacio Municipal on the Grand Plaza is site of traditional dances by the Ballet Folklórico de Mérida and Vaqueria Regional music by Orchestra Jaranera. Performers are both children and adults in traditional dress. Many of the dances involved trays of bottles or glasses balanced on the head. Free.

TUESDAY

Auditorio Olimpio, SW corner of the Plaza, showcases various musicians of Trova, the signature musical style of the region. 8:30pm. Free.

Parque Santiago at Calles 59 and 72 presents the Municipal Orchestra playing Big Band music of the US and Latin America such as Chacha, Mambo and Salsa. 9pm. Free.

WEDNESDAY

9pm. Teatro Peón Contreras, Calles 60 x 59 y 57, hosts the University of Yucatán Ballet Folklórico. M$50.
Auditorio Olimpio on the NW corner of the Plaza presents live music and performances. 9pm. Free.

THURSDAY

The Jaranera Orchestra plays Big Band music for dancing. Parque Zoologico del Centenario, Calle 59 y Avenida Itzaes. 4pm. Free.

Parque Santa Lucia, Calles 60 y 55, hosts the Serenata Yucateca presenting music of the region, dancing and other performances. 9pm. Free.

FRIDAY

Caribbean dance and music is offered in a different neighborhood park each week. 8pm. Free

In the courtyard of the University of Yucatán, Calles 60 y 57, the University of Yucatán Ballet Folklórico presents the dances of the region. 9pm.

SATURDAY

At 8pm the park at Paseo de Montejo and Calle 47 features Noche Mexicana, an offering of various regional and national musicians. Craft and food stands surround the area. Free.

At 9pm many of the streets leading to the Grand Plaza are closed. Restaurants set up tables in the streets and musicians and performers wander the streets. Free.

SUNDAY

Bici-Ruta From 8am – 12:30pm the city offers a bicycle route on closed-off streets through the city. Different stops along the route present various activities. Free. www.merida.gob.mx/biciruta/

Mérida en Domingo: Calle 60 from the Grand Plaza to Parque Santa Lucia is closed to traffic and various stalls set up for vendors of food, crafts and antiques. Families stroll through the city and live music and dancing is set up in various places. 9am – 9pm. Free

CITY GOVERNMENT OF MERIDA
Calle 59 x 52 y 50, Downtown Area 52-999-928-19-66/52-999-924-73-81
www.merida.gob.mx/turismo/
The Merida Tourism Office is where you can find all the information you need on new daily events, historical sites, geographical maps, weather, culture, attraction, demography, and other miscellaneous information. It does have the option to have the site in English in the upper right hand corner.

SECRETARIA DE LA CULTURA Y LAS ARTES
Calle 18 #204 x 23 y 25, Merida: 52-999-942-3800
The Ministry of Culture and the Arts helps contribute and develop cultural events and activities. These pertain to Dance, Theater, Music, Literature, Visual Arts, teaching art, popular culture, alternative youth demonstrations, food, historical research, publishing and promoting reading in order to preserve traditions. This website is in Spanish.

CASA CATHERWOOD
Calle 59 #572 y 72, Colonia Centro: 52-999-154-5565/ 917-880-8587
www.casa-catherwood.com
A collection of etchings of the Yucatán by English artist Frederick Catherwood. In the mid 1800s English adventurer and author John Lloyd Stephens toured the Yucatán Peninsula with his friend Catherwood. Stephens wrote a book of their excursions entitled Incidents of Travel in Yucatán, which was richly illustrated with etchings of the Mayan Ruins by Catherwood. The book ignited popular interest in Mayan archeology.

CASA DE MONTEJO
Calle 63 #506, Colonia Centro, Mérida: 999-923-0633
www.museocasamontejo.com
WEBSITE DOWN AT PRESSTIME
On the south side of the Grand Plaza you'll find the oldest structure in the city, currently a museum, originally built by the Spanish conqueror Francisco Montejo way back in the 1540s. On the façade you can see a vivid example of the violent history of the Yucatan: a carving of Spaniards standing on the heads of some unlucky Mayans, an example of how they defeated the natives. (Just a few miles to the north, the Americans were giving their Indians the same treatment. The only difference is that here the Indian

culture is intertwined with the modern world, so has not been wiped off the face of the earth, as it pretty much has in the U.S.) The gift shop here offers some of the best local crafts you can find in the area. It's curious to note that up until the 1970s the founding family of Mérida still occupied this house. Several of the front rooms are preserved in their colonial splendor and are open to the public during business hours. There is also one gallery which features excellently curated revolving exhibitions.

CASA MUSEO MONTES MOLINA
Calle 56 A #469 x 33 y 35, Merida: 52-999-925-5999
www.laquintamm.com
This mansion is an excellent example of the over-the-top Beaux Arts style that dominated the area in the early 1900's. The house is grand inside and out and a

guided tour offers glimpses of life in a mansion from top to bottom.
Mon – Fri, Business Hours, M$50

CATEDRAL DE SAN ILDEFONSO
Calle 60 x 61 y 57A, Centro, Merida, 999-255-8622
The Cathedral, located prominently on east side of the plaza, is the oldest found in the New World. Construction began in 1562 used the limestone from the dismantled Mayan temple which stood at the same site. The building is striking in its simplicity, lacking the ornamentation normally expected in colonial catholic cathedrals. Pillaging during the revolution of 1915 left the interior even more devoid of artifice. In the upper left corner of the sanctuary lies a small chapel where hangs Cristo de las Ampollas (Christ of the Blisters). The story goes that crucifix was carved from a tree in the town of Ichmul burned all night and showed no sign of damage. In 1645 the Ichmul church itself burned down, but the statue survived,

though blistered. Opinions differ as to whether the statue disappeared in 1915 and a replacement was put in its place. The statue is the center of a local fiesta which lasts from mid-September to mid-October.

GRAND PLAZA

Calle 50 #460, Frac. Gonzálo Guerrero, Merida: 52-999-944-7658

www.granplaza.com.mx/directorio

Mérida's cultural life centers around the Grand Plaza, or Plaza de la Independencia. If the late afternoon and evening the plaza becomes filled with people enjoying the fine weather and social interaction. Here we find couples unabashedly kissing away next to little of ladies chatting away. Groups of friends huddle around laptops, for the plaza – like all the plazas in town – offers free WiFi (which we think is terribly civilized). Many vendors patrol the plaza, most noticeably the young Mayan women, dressed in their traditional outfits, offering a large selection of their lovely textiles. Free concerts featuring local and national artists are sometimes offered in the plaza.

HACIENDA YAXCOPOIL

Federla Hwy. 261, km 186, Mérida: 52-999-900-1193

www.yaxcopoil.com

For a real trip into the past, hire a driver (make sure he speaks English) for the half-hour drive out here. This is one of the most significant henequen plantations in the area. It's a hue place and an architectural wonder. It once covered over 22,000 acres. (Henequen was converted into rope from the agave plant and shipped round the world, bringing in huge amounts of money to Mexico.) This hacienda dates back to the 17th century and they have done a very good job keeping the original look of the place. It looks very lived in. you can even visit the machine shop where the rope was made. (The machine still works, though production was halted in 1984.) What's really great about this place is that it's run as a private concern. It's not as spic and span as more touristy places. Plus, a visit here really gets you out into the country, something it's much safer to do in Mérida than in other parts of Mexico.

LA TERCERA ORDEN

Calle 60 x 59, Merida: 52-999-924-9712

Small church constructed in 1618 by the Jesuits. Check to see if there's a wedding or a quinceañera schedule while you're in town. It's fun to watch these colorful ceremonies if you're lucky enough to see one going on.

MUSEO DE ARTE CONTEMPORÁNEO ATENEO DE YUCATÁN

Calle 60 #502 B, Centro: 52-999-928-3258
Located on the east side of the plaza next to the Cathedral, the museum – shortened to MACAY – boasts a very impressive collection of modern art. The permanent collection is filled with work by many of the internationally recognized artists from the south of Mexico. The many galleries of the museum also regularly house traveling exhibitions both national and international. We highly recommend a visit.

MUSEO REGIONAL DE ANTROPOLOGÍA

Paseo de Montejo #485 & Calle 43, Mérida: 52-999-923-0469/ 52-999-923-0557
www.palaciocanton.inah.gob.mx
Housed in the Paseo de Montejo's **Palacio Cantón**, the mansion built by railroad baron and former governor General Francisco Cantón, the museum offers an excellent background to understanding the history and culture of the Mayan Civilization and the region in general. There are exhibits covering pre-history all the way up to the present. Here we get some fascinating insight in to the regular life of the Maya. Of particular fascination is the exhibit, complete with skulls, showing the Mayan fascination with elongating the cranium by tying boards to the heads of babies. On Sunday, they close the street from 8 a.m. to 12:30 p.m. for cyclists. You can hire a

bike for just a few pesos at the corner of 62nd and 63rd Streets in the city administration building. Or ask someone.

MUSEO DE ARTE POPULAR DE YUCATÁN
Calle 50-A #487 x 57, Centro Histórico: 52-999-928-5263
NO WEBSITE
This small museum offers an excellent retrospective on the rich and varied Mexican arts and crafts of the region. It also has a little gift shop offering high-quality work.

MUSEO DE LA CANCIÓN YUCATECA
Calle 57 #464 y 48, Parque de la Mejorada: 52-999-923-7224
www.museodelacancionyucateca.com

Here we have a nice collection of memorabilia of the rich and varied musical traditions of the Yucatán Peninsula. The gift shop has a great selection of cds.

MUSEO DE LA CIUDAD

Calle 56 #529a x 65 y 65a, Centro: 52-999-924-4264
www.merida.gob.mx
Two galleries feature a mish-mash of artifacts and exhibits relating to the City of Mérida, its history and important public figures.

PALACIO DE GOBERNADOR (GOVERNOR'S PALACE)

Calle 60 s/n X calle 61 y 59, Centro: 52-999-930-3100
The state administrative offices are housed in this 19th century building on the northeast corner of the Grand Plaza. The walls are covered in murals by the modernist (and Mérida -born) Fernando Castro Pacheco, showing the adversities faced by the Mayan people since their subjugation by invading Europeans.

PASEO DE MONTEJO

In the 19th century, the world demand for the sisal fibers of the henequen plant made fortunes for the landed families of the Yucatán. Always looking for Europe for inspiration, these neuvo-richer decided to create a wide boulevard north of the center of town where they could build their grand mansions. Thus came into being the Paseo de Montejo. A series of Beaux Arts manors, each attempting to out-do the last, was built along the street, which fancied itself a new-world Champs de Ellisei. The result is debatable. Personally we find most of these structures to be pretentious and out of place. But they are certainly interesting to look at, and there are some nice examples. Today most of these building are occupied by companies.

Chapter 6
EXCURSIONS

RUINS

It would be a shame to visit the Yucatán and not see Mayan Ruins. There are hundreds of known Mayan ruins. We list here the ones most convenient to visitors to Mérida. Take bug spray and plenty of water. And you might want to take some bananas to feed the ubiquitous iguanas.

UXMAL

About an hour south of Mérida, Uxmal (pronounced Oosh-Mal) is a UNESCO World Heritage Site, and an excellent example of the sophistication of the Mayan Civilization. In size and scope it rivals the great sites such as Chichén Itzá, but it doesn't have the masses of people, so one feels more intimately connected with the beautiful architecture. And unlike Chichén Itzá, you can still climb one of the pyramids. Bring plenty of water, because it gets quite hot, and bottled water on site is pricey.

RUTA PUUC

The Ruta Puuc is the name of the route south of Mérida that takes in a series of well-preserved Mayan ruins. The entire route can be taken in a day. Heading an hour south of Mérida, the first and most well-known is Uxmal. After Uxmal the route hits the lesser-known sites of Kabáh, Sayil, Xlapak, and Labná. These sites are all well-preserved and each offers its unique flavor and ambience. Along the route are also other sites of interest such as henequen haciendas, cenotes and cave systems.

DZIBILCHALTÚN

These ruins the distinction of being the longest continuously inhabited of any known Mayan city, from 1000 BC right up until the Spanish occupation. There are thousands of buildings mapped in the area. Unfortunately, most of them were dismantled and the materials used to construct the local towns and roads. But the main religious complex is still extant and still beautiful. Like Chichén Itzá the buildings are laid out with astronomical precision. There is also a Mayan museum and a Fraciscan chapel on site.

CHICHÉN ITZÁ

Chichén Itzá is the most popular Mayan site on the Yucatán peninsula. The site is listed as one of the Seven New Wonders of the World. It is a good distance from Cancún, but dozens of tour buses a day make the 2 ½ hour trek. We recommend having a guide for this site. Being the most famous and developed site, it is also the most restrictive. Visitors are not allowed in the buildings or to climb the pyramids. The guides provide a rich narrative to spark one's imagination and form a bond with the site. Excellent bilingual guides can be hired for a reasonable price at the entrance. Many visitors appreciate the mathematical accuracy and astrological alignment of the buildings. If possible, we recommend visiting on either the Spring or Fall Equinox, where you can join the thousands of people who come to watch the Descent of the Serpent, a shadow cast at just the right angle to create the appearance of a snake descending the Temple of Kukulcan. After a sweaty day of wandering around Chichen Itza, we recommend you cool off with a refreshing dip in Ik Kil cenote, a few kilometers away.

THE BEACH

Mérida proper is not on the ocean, so the beach is actually about half an hour away in the town of Progresso. Progresso is where the city flocks to in the summer to deal with the heat. Some people like to turn their nose up at Progresso. There is a huge deep-water pier sticking six kilometers out into the water, but we find it rather interesting. The beach is beautiful with warm water and white sand and a constant breeze makes even the hottest day pleasant. In the non-summer months Progresso turns into a sleepy village awoken only by the occasional cruise ship.

CELESTÚN

About an hour west of Mérida lies the town of Celestún, which has been made famous for the colonies of pink flamingoes that make it their home. The Ría Celestún Biosphere Reserve is host to these breathtaking birds year-around, and in the winter months migrating flocks of blue-winged teals and shovelers make it even more exciting. A thriving Eco-tourism industry has sprung up. Boat tours take visitors into the ría to visit the roosts and then to the sweet-water springs for swimming.

CENOTES

One interesting fact about the Yucatán Peninsula is that there are no rivers. For various geological and tectonic reasons, all water flows underground. The limestone rock covering reservoirs of water in many places has collapsed, leaving open-air sinkholes called Cenotes. These cenotes are often hundreds of feet deep, with crystal-clear cool water. Swimming in these cenotes is an interesting and exciting alternative to a day at the beach. We highly recommend you take at least one day to experience this uniquely Yucatecan pastime.

HACIENDAS

The country around Mérida is strewn with many old haciendas, some of them dating back to the seventeenth century when Spanish settlers claimed vast tracks of land for cattle-raising or farming. The golden age of the haciendas, though, was the latter part of the nineteenth century when the world demand for "sisal" created massive plantations of the henequen cactus it was made from. Sisal fiber was used in the making of ropes and twine. By the early twentieth century demand was receding, and with the advent of artificial fibers in the 1940s, the market dried up. But not before making massive fortunes for the local land-owners and producing the mansions on the Paseo de Montejo in Mérida. Most of the haciendas fell into dis-repair, and many are still deserted, but in recent years some have been renovated and turned into hotels and retreats. Some have been preserved in their original condition and here you can see the buildings and machines used in the processing of henequen fibers into sisal.

RENTING A CAR

Renting a car is a great way to explore the many opportunities Mérida and the Yucatán Peninsula has to offer. We recommend reserving your car ahead of time. When renting your car, it is very important that you specifically request insurance equal to the value of the car. It is not made clear when you pick up your car, but you are personally responsible for any damage to the car. Upon return you are at the mercy of the staff for any scratch, so be very aware of the condition of the vehicle when you get it.

Chapter 7
SHOPPING & SERVICES

Mérida is an excellent place to shop for a stunningly wide array of beautiful arts and crafts of the Yucatán region. The area around the **Grand Plaza**, particularly to the north, is filled with shops offering these wares. You've got to buy one of the traditional hand-embroidered costumes. Huipiles, still worn by women today, are striking embroidered tunic blouses. The top and bottom edges of the huipil are hand embroidered with figures in single and double cross stitch. These embroidered flowers, fruits, and birds represent the history of creation and, according to their creators, protect the wearer from negative energies.

EL AGUACATE
Calle 58 esq Calle 73 #604 Centro, Mérida: 52-999-947-4651
www.hamacaselaguacate.com.mx
Hammocks, hammocks, hammocks. From $20 up to the nicest ones at $200. Also a wide range of guayaberas, the dressy Cuban shirts with all the pockets. These shirts used to come from Cuba, but after Castro, locals created their own take on these great shirts. (You can get cheap polyester ones, but if you can afford it, go for a linen one, but it'll cost well over $100.) Not a good area to be in at night, so go by day.

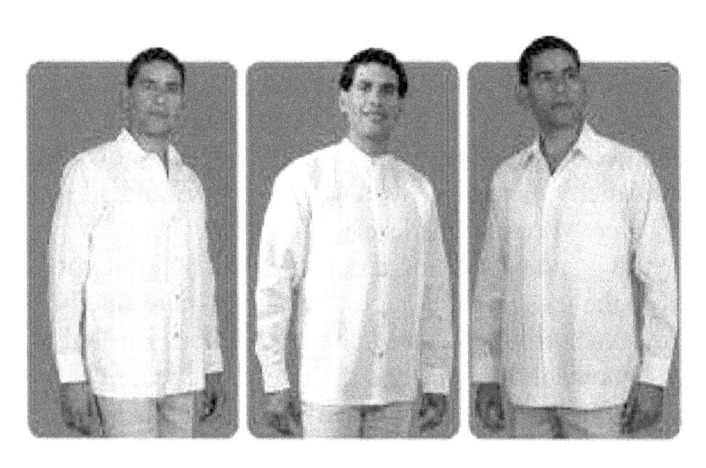

GUAYABERAS JACK
Calle 59 #507A x 60 y 62, Mérida: 52-999-928-5999
www.guayaberasjack.com.mx **WEBSITE DOWN**

I guess you can tell what the special item is here. If you can't afford the linen one, get an all-cotton.

MARKET

If you haven't been to a Latin American market, then you should go just as a cultural experience. The market is a sprawling series of indoor spaces covering several city blocks between Calles 65 – 69 and 54 – 56. Here you can wander narrow aisles where anything and everything is for sale. We suggest you avoid the meat area, though – it can get quite smelly. The area surrounding the market for blocks is filled with shops of all kinds and the crowd is thick.

Hammocks – Mérida is known for the handmade hammocks of the region. Due to the heat, most locals sleep in hammocks. These hammocks are inexpensive, about M$250, and lightweight, so they make an ideal and useful souvenir to take back with you. We recommend you avoid the super-cheap ones sold on the street, as the quality is poor.

Panama Hats – These hats are handmade in several towns to the south of Mérida. They are made from the fibers of the jipijapa palm and woven in caves to keep the fibers moist. The hats sold in Mérida are of good quality and very well-priced. A variety of styles are available. Look around and try many styles until you have found the one that's just right for you.
Guayaberas – Mérida and Cuba fight over bragging rights as the birthplace of the guayabera. These lightweight short-sleeve mens shirts are the business and dress attire of this tropical area. Shops offer a selection of styles and materials. We recommend cotton or linen.
Huipiles – These traditional womens' blouses are decorated in bright embroidery and feature a variety of colorful motifs and styles.
Coconut Sweets – The region is known for its coconut candies. Many different local fruits and delicacies are combined to make these tasty confections an irresistible treat.

INDEX

W

How About Some Free Thrillers?

Besides his travel & restautant guides, the author also writes page-turning political thrillers.

Send him an email and he'll send you the **first 3** in his bestselling series **FREE**.

Why, you ask, would he do something so foolish?

Because he's sure he'll get you hooked.

andrewdelaplaine@mac.com